Business Plan Template
Learn the Simple Truth of How to Create an Effective Business Plan

Table of Contents

Introduction

Chapter 1: Before Writing Your Plan

Chapter 2: Writing Your Business Plan

Chapter 3: Tips and Tricks

Chapter 4: SMART Business Planning

Chapter 5: The Purpose of Niches

Conclusion

Introduction

Thank you for purchasing *"Business Plan Template:* Learn the Simple Truth of How to Create an Effective Business Plan". Before you get started, we want to congratulate you on having an amazing business idea that you are dedicated to. The first step in business is having a phenomenal idea, and the second step is creating a strong plan to back your idea up and turn it into a reality!

At this point, you probably have the perfect idea to launch a business. You have invested tons of time into planning out the details like how you will serve people, the way your products or services will enhance people's lives, and why your idea is cutting edge and at the forefront of market trends. You have dreamt of all of the ways you will use this idea to lead you to success, and develop a business that sets you apart from the competition and makes you a leader in the marketing world. But, before you can get started, you need to get the business plan written down. You need a solid plan that will help you present your brilliant idea to others, and help them see exactly why your idea is so amazing. Then, you can get all of the support you need to turn your incredible business idea into an action plan that gets results.

In order to achieve these results, you need a business plan. Not just any business plan, though, you need *the best business plan.* One that converts your amazing ideas into viable information backed by research that proves why your business is *the* business that people should invest their time and money into. If you are looking to have a business plan as sharp as your business idea, you have come to the right place. In this book, we are going to turn your amazing idea into a feasible action plan that will take you to the top of your industry. Business plans are an incredible tool in helping you get important supports in place for your budding company, as well as to provide you with a clear action plan to take you to the top – and what to do if your action plan is not working to its highest abilities.

If you are ready to turn your amazing dream into a reality, then you need to take the very first step and start your business plan. In order to seek the best results from your business plan, you will need to pay close attention to the information in this book, and invest some time in putting together the best plan you have ever dreamed of. Your phenomenal idea combined with our amazing business planning talents are all you need to create a business plan that will emerge your business into the real world.

Chapter 1: Before Writing Your Plan

Before you get that amazing idea in action, you need to get your wits about you! A business plan is an excellent tool to help you have focus and drive when you are launching and running your business. This nifty little tool will have you take action in your business that will drive you forward towards your goals, as well as lead incredible presentations to secure the support you need to get your business off the ground!

The gist of a business plan is simple: create an action plan that will help you launch your business. The reality is, there is more to it than that. Business plans require some preparation work in order to help you create a solid business plan that will drive home your successes! It isn't enough to merely slap together some information you discovered on a quick internet search and call it a day. No, you need to conduct real research to get real numbers that support your business and help you create a solid foundation for the plan on which your business will run. Before you dive into filling out your business plan, you need to lay some important groundwork, first.

Nail Down the Basics

If you are an entrepreneur, you have probably thought up exactly what you dream for your company in regards to what your idea and vision is. However, you may not have considered other elements such as the legal structure, budget, market interests, or other important conditions that come into play when you are starting a business. It is important to take a look into all of this before you put together a business plan, so that you completely understand what you are doing and where you are going.

Legal Structure

There are a few elements that come into play when it comes to the legal structure of your business. Depending on what you are doing and what your intention is, you will want to decide how your business will be identified. Will you be a sole proprietorship, a partnership, or a corporation? Once you discover which you want to be, it will be easier to understand what legal steps you need to take in order to complete that goal. For example, you will need to register your business name and receive a business number if you want to run a sole proprietorship, and if you want to run a corporation you will need a corporation number plus a completed application to apply for your corporation.

Budget
Many people get excited about what they are going to do in the way of their business, but fail to think about how the budget will work. When you are running a business, the budget is critical to your success. If you fail to look at the finances of your company, there is a good chance that your company won't succeed. Start-ups tend to be costlier than month-to-month business maintenance fees, so you will need to consider all of the costs of your start up. For example, you will have to pay to register your business and receive your business or incorporation number, you will need to pay for marketing and advertising, you may need to pay employees or sign a lease and pay a security deposit on top of your rental fee, you may need to invest in initial stock, and much more. Depending on what your business is, you will have to consider all of the startup requirements and their associated fees. That way you can create a clear budget and you know what you are asking for or looking to raise when you are preparing to acquire your start-up costs.

Market Research
You really need to make sure that you research your intended market and understand what you are entering. Sometimes, you may have a wonderful idea but unless you can directly compete with a flooded industry, it may not be worth following that idea. Or, you may just need to create a stronger edge so you are of greater competition to the rest. There are many ways you can combat a flooded industry, but you need to make sure that you can *definitely* compete with others in the industry. A good way to avoid this problem is to focus on niche areas and have a very specific targeted

audience. It may feel like you are reducing your audience, but the reality is you are actually increasing your potential market. There is a saying that states "when you speak to everyone, no one listens, but if you speak to one crowd, the whole room hears you." This is especially important to focus on when you are building a business. To start, you should choose a niche (or a few) and then thoroughly research them to see which your business would be most successful in and who you can serve the most.

Research Your Route to Market
Your route to the market is essentially how you intend to enter the market in order to be seen and "hit the ground running". As a new entrepreneur you should focus on having a single high-impact route as opposed to a multi-channel route, as it can be extremely costly to go through too many channels and could wind up in you having lower quality impact due to limited budget. Instead, if you focus your budget and entrance on one area, you can have a higher-impact and receive better quality returns on your marketing investment than you might have otherwise. In order to pick a high-impact route, you will need to be clear on who your target audience is. Then, you can conduct appropriate research to discover what marketing strategies have the highest impact on reaching your target audience by attracting their attention and converting them from leads into customers.

Understand How You Benefit Your Customer
Having a great idea is wonderful, but if customers don't understand why your idea is so great for *them* they will probably not invest their money into your product or service. Instead of putting excessive emphasis on the service or your business, take a significant amount of time to understand what the customer needs and how you can effectively serve those needs. Make sure your products and services reflect what they are looking for, and have a strong understanding of how your product or service is a positive impact on their lives and why investing in it would benefit them. The more you emphasize on the customer, the easier it will be to

effectively interact with your target audience and turn leads into actual business.

Mentors Can Help!
Many business owners like to outsource some of their tasks so that they don't have to focus on everything all on their own. If you are considering hiring help, one of the people you should consider hiring is a business mentor. These are people who have already been through the steps and who can help ensure you take all of the appropriate action to structure your business plan. They can also help you with the foundation of your entire business in the most effective way so you have a higher impact and less chances of your foundation being cracked or falling through entirely. Mentors for businesses come in many shapes and sizes, with most specializing in their own specific niches. It can be beneficial to look where you could use help the most and then see if there are any mentors or business coaches available to you who specialize in that category. While it may seem like a large investment up front, having someone who can help you perfect your foundation and launch into your business with their own expertise and knowledge on the industry can be extremely helpful.

Follow This Book!
In addition to all of the above, you should make sure you carefully follow the instructions in this book. This book is the perfect guide to help you completely design your business plan so that you have thought through every aspect and have a solid foundation to operate from. Each section, step and tip is dedicated to ensuring that you have a thorough business plan that looks as though you hired a professional to write it for you. The more time you invest in each step and complete the process entirely, the more successful your plan will be and the easier it will be to launch your business with it.

When you take the time to lay a strong foundation for your business plan, you ensure that you will have every element thought out. The more detailed and sound your foundation is, the stronger your business plan will be and the much easier it will be to launch a successful business. In order to run a business, you really need to have all levels of information available to you in order to make decisions that will have a positive impact on your company. If you fail to consider every aspect of your business, you are going to end up neglecting areas and as a result these areas can end up suffering and cripple the foundation of your business. This type of tragedy is very common and is why about 50 percent of all new business startups fail in the first four to five years of business. To prevent this from happening, *make sure you lay the ground work.*

Chapter 2: Writing Your Business Plan

So you know your idea so intimately that you can explain it inside and out, front to back and back to front. You have put in the necessary work to figure out the basics and lay a strong foundation for your business plan, which will ultimately lay the foundation for your entire business. You haven't put it all together yet, but you are clear on the majority of the basics revolving around your business startup. Now what?

Well, now it's time to write the business plan, of course!

While your business plan may vary slightly depending on what model of business you are launching (online, offline, larger, or smaller), virtually all business plans still require the same information to be present. Ideally, you are going to explore and explain topics including: legal structure, employees, target customers, services, growth strategies, exit strategies, and more. All of this information is incredibly important when it comes to planning a business because without it, you may not have any idea how a certain aspect of your business should operate in order to succeed. Then, you may not end up taking the correct action in order to see that area thrive and it could fade instead, causing your business foundation to become weak and potentially cripple your entire business. Instead of making this common mistake, ensure you invest enough time into your business plan to make sure you are well aware of how all areas of your business should run in order to be successful.

In this chapter, we are going to explore exactly how you should write your business plan. We are going to cover every topic that your business plan should include, learn about why it is important to be in your plan, and help you structure your business plan so that it is professional and provides you with a wonderful opportunity to request support or funding from people if required.

The Elements of a Business Plan

In total, there are nine different sections that your business plan should include. Each section is devoted to a part of your businesses foundation, and will help you clearly present your business plan to others. All areas of your business plan are equally important when it comes to having a solid foundation for your business, so make sure you invest plenty time in each area to ensure it contains plenty of factual and compelling information to help you present your plan later on. The more work you do now, the less you will need to do later. In addition to that, the more professional and qualified your business plan is, the easier it will be to request funding or additional support in the future.

Executive Summary

This brief summary is an opportunity to explain where your company currently is in the market, where you intend to take it, and explains why your business idea will be a success. This section is especially important if you are seeking funding, as it will immediately help you capture your potential investors' interests.

When you are writing your executive summary, you need to highlight the strengths of your overall business plan. It should be the very last section you write, but the first section you present in your plan.

There are many things to include in the executive summary that will help it serve its purpose successfully by capturing the attention of potential investors. Below are some things you should include in your executive summary:

- Company Mission Statement: The purpose of your business, explained in a paragraph or less.
- Important Company Information: A brief statement that indicates when your business was founded, the names of the founders and their roles in the company, the number of employees, and where your business is located.

- Highlighted Growth: Provide evidence of your company growth, including financial or market highlights if available. You can use graphs or charts as helpful visual aids.
- Services or Products: Give a brief description of what your company provides.
- Current Financial Information: If you are requesting financing, include any relevant information about your current bank as well as existing investors.
- Brief Plans for Future: Summarize where you intend to take your business in the future.

If you are in the process of starting a new business, you won't have any existing information on how your business is performing yet. Instead, you can provide information on your credentials and why you are suited to run a business of this type. You can also provide any relevant information or summaries proving your existing success and why you will be able to turn the business into a profitable, successful empire.

Company Description
While this might sound similar to the executive description, it is actually quite a bit different. In the executive description, you should have already provided basic information including your existing position in the marketplace, your physical location and size, and more. The company description itself is a lot deeper than this, however. In this section you are going to provide a review of the various elements of your business. This is an opportunity to quickly explain the goal of your business and why you are unique.

The company description section should include information such as:
- The nature of the business you are running or starting.
- All of the different marketplace needs you are intending to satisfy.

- A detailed description of your target audience, whether it is a consumer, organization or business
- Competitive advantages that your business has which will make it a success (i.e. location, experts, more efficient operations, or the ability to bring great value to customers.)

Market Analysis

This is an incredible opportunity for you to understand how your intended market works and how you can fit into it. For this section you are going to be researching your target audience and gaining information on how they consume products and how you can use their behavioral patterns to benefit the success of your business. While this information is important to any potential investors, it is also extremely important to you. Having a clear understanding of your target audience and what makes them purchase product is going to help you create strong campaigns that reach and capture the attention of your targeted audience. Then, the rest of your business will be responsible for attracting their business and engaging in your products or services.

When you are completing the market analysis of your business plan, you should take some time and really focus on doing thorough research. There are actually businesses out there who will help you with this, but you can also do it yourself if you are willing to invest the time into it. The information you will need to research and discuss includes:

- Description of Industry: Clearly describe your industry, including information such as its current size, previous growth rates, and other important characteristics or trends (such as: life cycle stage, etc.)
- Industry Outlook: You will also want to take the time to understand the future of your industry and ensure that it is growing at a rapid enough rate that you will be able to jump in and make money.

- Target Audience: You need to get clear on your niche and narrow it down to a manageable size. There is a saying: if you speak to the whole room, no one will listen to you. This is true when you are creating a business. Make sure you have a specific audience you are talking to so that you know exactly who you are trying to appeal to and can easily find out how to do that.
- Important Characteristics: Specifically understand the important needs of your potential customers, and whether or not those needs are being met. Also take the time to understand how exactly your company can meet those needs, better than other companies already are if that is applicable. You should also discover what your exact demographics are and where you can find them. If there are any seasonal purchasing trends they generally partake in, you should also take the time to learn how that will impact your business.
- Target Audience Size: In addition to understanding the size of your industry, you also need to understand the size of your own niche. Include any data that you can pertaining to the annual purchases made, the forecasted growth rate, and anything else pertaining to your business.
- Audience Reach: Naturally, not the entire audience is going to take the bait. You need to invest some time in figuring out approximately how much of that audience will actually do business with you in a defined geographic area. You also need to explain the logic behind your calculations.
- Define Pricing and Gross Margin: You need to get clear on your pricing structure, as well as your gross margin levels. If you are going to use any discounts, you should also include information regarding these.
- Analyze the Competition: You need to make sure you keep a clear eye on the competition so you can stay ahead of them and ensure your business has a competitive edge. This information should include:
    - The competitors' products or services

- Where they fit in the competing market
- Their market shares
- Any strengths and weaknesses they have
- The importance of your target market to your competitors
- If they impose any barriers that may affect your entrance in the market
- Where your window of opportunity is in the market in comparison to your competitors
- Any secondary or indirect competitors that may exist and impact the success of your business
- If there are any barriers to the market (ex. Costly investments, evolving technology, etc.)
- Regulations: You should also include any regulatory requirements from customers or governments. If these regulations affect your business, you should outline how you will comply. You should also include any information about how the regulations will impact your business.

When you are completing this segment of your business plan, you should only include information that comes from the results of any testing you conduct. You do not need to provide information on how you came to these conclusions in this section. Instead, you can include all of that information in the appendix. This will keep this section f your business plan clear and to-the-point.

Organization and Management
This important section of your business plan is dedicated to describing the management structure of your company. Here, you can share details such as who owns the company, a profile of the company's management team, and all of the qualifications held by your board of directors.

The questions you will be answering here include: Who has what responsibilities in the company? What background do they hold and why have you chosen them for their position? What exact responsibilities do they have? While you may not find these questions important, any potential investors are going to want to know this information since your company's organization and management plays a vital role in its success. You may have a great idea, but if you don't have qualified individuals supporting it, you will not have the manpower needed to make your idea work.

The easiest way to complete this section is to create a chart that will help you organize everyone. This way, you can prove you've thought out every element of the management team and that you are not leaving anything to chance. This ensures that everything will be done properly and effectively, and that any investors or potential employees will not have to worry about anything being left incomplete or being completed several times over before it is actually done.

You need to include the following information in this section, somewhere on your organizational chart:
- All of the owners, including their names and their percentage of ownership
- How involved each of the owners are with the company
- What forms of ownership exist (i.e. preferred stock, common stock, limited liability partnership, etc.)
- Any outstanding equity equivalents
- Common stock (ex. Issued or authorized)
- The profiles of management
- The expertise of the key people in your company and their backgrounds. Include the resumes of these key people with the following information on them:
    - Full Name
    - Position Title and Primary Duties
    - All Education
    - Individuals' Skills and Experience
    - Previous Employment
    - Unique Skills

- Track Record
- Recognition Within' the Industry
- Involvement in Community
- Length of Time Spent with Company
- Compensation
- Quantifiable Achievements

In addition to including the proper people, you need to explain how these people highlight your own skills and expertise. If you are a new company on the scene, you can instead describe how these individuals will accentuate your expertise and contribute to the success of your business.

Having a board of directors is a great opportunity to have an unpaid advisory board that provides expertise that your company may not be able to afford otherwise. If you have one, present a list of well-known, successful business owners and managers to help contribute to the credibility of your company and the perception of your management expertise. If you operate your business with a board of directors, you should gather the following information for your business plan, in addition to the above information:

- Names of People Involved
- Board Position
- Company Involvement
- Unique Background
- Previous Contributions to Company's Success
- Projected Contributions to Company's Success

Services or Product Lines
This is the section where you get the opportunity to let your incredible business idea shine. It is likely that your entire idea sprouted from a single inspiration to have a special service or product line to offer on the market. Most businesses start out with the idea of a service or product, and grow into major businesses from there. In this section, you are going to describe what your

product or service is, highlight the benefits it has for potential and current (if applicable) clients, and why your product or service will fill a need for your target consumers.

In this section, you might feel compelled to ramble on about the various benefits of your product or service. While it is important to provide detailed information, you need to also make sure that you provide it in a professional way that is consumable by those who will be seeing or reading your business proposal. To ensure this section doesn't become muddled or actually detract from the quality of your business plan, make sure you follow the following tips carefully to create a well-structured and professional looking business plan describing all of the reasons why your particular product or service is so incredible and why you stand behind it:

- Detailed Description of Product or Service: Here is where you get to let your idea shine! You now have an opportunity to share a detailed description of the product or service that was the basis for your entire business plan. You need to include specific benefits about your product or service from the perspective of your customer, *not* from your own perspective. You also need to talk about how your product or service can meet your targeted consumer's needs, any and all advantages that your product or service has over the competition, and what stage your product or service is currently in (i.e. prototype).
- Detailed Product Life Cycle: You should include information about where your product or service is currently at in its life cycle. So, if the type of product you're providing has already been on the market for a while, you need to explain how far along in its cycle it is, and justify why it is a good idea for you to enter the market now with this product. You should also include information that may affect or influence the future of the products life cycle.
- Intellectual Property: It is important to share any information regarding existing, pending, or anticipated copyrights or patent filings. You should also share whether

your product has any key aspects that are classified as trade secrets. Finally, you should include any information that pertains to existing legal agreements surrounding your product or service, such as nondisclosure or non-compete agreements.
- Research and Development Activities (R&D Activities): You should take the time to emphasize and touch base on any research and development activities your company has taken on to ensure your product is at the top of its class. In addition to analyzing your own company's efforts, you should also take a look at the activities of others in your targeted industry.

Having a clear and structured description of your product or service that highlights why it is so amazing is ultimately what is going to allow you to tell people what your company is all about. Having an incredible business structure is important, but it is only important if you have a high quality product or service to provide to the market. In this section, you really need to let the authenticity and uniqueness of your product shine through as you're sharing why your product or service is worth investing in. While you don't want to get sloppy or lose your professional edge, you still need to make sure that you really fuel this section with all of the reasons why your company will shine through the products and/or services you will have to offer.

Marketing and Sales
Now that you have effectively researched your target audience, their consumer habits, and how your product can fulfill those needs, you need to take some time to research marketing and sales. This section of your business plan should focus solely on your marketing strategies and sales management in order to oversee success in your business.

Successful marketing will help you create customers, which are the backbone of your entire business. When you are working on the marketing and sales section of your business plan, you first need to focus on the marketing strategies you will implement. There are various ways you can approach the marketing element of your business, exactly how is going to largely depend on who your target audience is and what their consumerism behavior is like. There are, however, common steps you can take which will help you work through the direction and tactics you want to use to drive sales and create customer loyalty.

A successful marketing strategy should include:
- An entrance strategy (how you will enter the market)
- Growth strategies (how you intend to grow your business, internally and externally for the greater benefit of overall business growth)
- Distribution channels strategy (how you intend to distribute your services or products)
- Communication strategy (how you will reach your customers, what variety of marketing strategies you will use to effectively reach them such as advertisements, promotions, etc.)

Following the development of a comprehensive and informative marketing strategy, you should look to make a sales strategy. While the marketing strategy states how you intend to attract customers, the sales strategy focuses on how exactly you intend to sell to these customers. Your sales strategy needs these two elements in order to be successful:
- Sales force (a sales force is the individuals who are actually conducting the sales. For example, will you have internal representatives or independent representatives? You should also consider how many sales people your force will have, recruitment strategies, training strategies, and ideal compensation plans.)

- Sales activities (this is a productivity list that will essentially tell the sales force how to spend their time. They should spend their time doing sales-generating tasks such as: making calls, developing customer relationships, selling, turning leads into customers, reaching sales targets, and more.)

Requesting Funding

If you are not intending to request funding for your business, you likely won't need this part of the plan included. For some people, they are using their business plan as an opportunity to outline company growth, or have a clear vision to share with potential employees. However, for many businesses, especially startups or ones undergoing significant growth, requesting funding is one of the primary purposes for having a solid business plan in effect. If you are seeking to request funding for the purpose of starting or growing your business, then you will want to add this section.

Outlying your funding request is going to be the same regardless of what your business model is. The information you will need to include, and the format it needs to be presented in needs to be generally the same. Remember, you will want to be professional and appealing, as well as clear and honest. Potential investors want to make sure you are trustworthy and that you are clear and focused on what you are doing, as they do not want to waste their money on someone who is not going to make use of it in the best possible way.

When you are generating your funding request, here is the information you need to include:
- What your exact request is (how much funding do you need?)
- Any funding requirements you may have over the next five years (so they can be aware as to whether or not they might

need to invest more further down the line, or share their investors position with other investors.)
- How you plan to use the funding (you need to be clear on what the funding is for: working capital, acquisitions, debt retirement, etc.)
- Strategic financial situational plans for the future (i.e. buyout, debt repayment plan, being acquired, or even selling your business.)

All of the aforementioned points absolutely have to be expressed in your business plan, for each of them directly relates to the funding you would receive. In some cases, the circumstances affect your repayment abilities, which is crucial for investors to know so that they can be well aware in advance as to what your intentions are with your investor relationship.

When you are creating your funding requirements, you should ensure that you clearly outline what you are requesting now, and what you are requesting for the future. Because of this, you will need to project your growth rate and develop intentions for how you plan for your business to grow within' the next five years. This gives investors the opportunity to decide whether or not they can afford *all* of the funding you are asking for, or if they will need to share the investors position with another investor down the line. In addition, you will need to outline the time period that the funding will cover, and what specific terms you would like applied to the funding.

In addition to providing information about what you need and for the future, you should also include information that supports your repayment abilities. Historical financial information and growth, if available, is a great opportunity to prove your ability to repay the investment, and therefore should be included. Investors will want to know that you are able to return their capital, and that they are not investing in something that will lose them money.

Financial Projections

This section of your business plan allows you to allocate money based on the information you've researched and gathered previously throughout your planning stages. In the financial projections section, you can take the combined knowledge of your analyzed market and clear objectives, and then allocate resources in order to effectively meet your goals. When you are completing the financial projections part of your business plan, you should include historical financial data and prospective financial data.

If you have already owned an established business for a while, you will have historical financial data which you will need to supply. This data will clearly show the financial trends and performance of your company. The majority of creditors will want to see the last three to five years of your financial data, as well as be made aware of any collateral you may have that could be used to ensure your loan. This can happen at any stage of your business, whether you are new or have been in business for a while. It is important to have this information handy so you are prepared when this phase of the financial planning comes along. Being prepared will help ensure you have everything available that might be requested, and will further assist you in your case of requesting funding.

In addition to historic data, you will need to have your prospective financial data in place. If you are a startup, this is going to be the area you will focus most on. This section essentially allows you to share how you expect your company to be performing in the next five years. You should be as detailed as possible, and also make it clear how you came to this conclusion. You should do these for each year up to five years. For the first year, you should do monthly or quarterly expectations of growth, and remaining four years you can do quarterly and/or annual ones. In these projections you should include: expected income statements, cash flow statements, capital expenditure budgets and balance sheets.

When you are requesting funding, you need to ensure that your financial projections match your funding requests. Creditors are going to want to make sure that there are no inconsistencies, and will be much less likely to offer you money if there are any. It is better for you to catch these mistakes as opposed to them catching them, because if they do it can be detrimental to your ability to receive funding. In addition, make sure you back up all of the assumptions you make in your claims so that the creditor will not be left guessing, and you with no answer.

You will also want to include a short analysis of your financial information. For this you will want to have included a ratio and trend analysis which will account for all of your financial statements, both prospective *and* historical. It can also be beneficial to add graphs to this section to help explain your growth expectations.

Appendix
While an appendix is not mandatory in a business plan, it can definitely be beneficial to include. This allows you to tie up any loose ends and explain anything where there was not room to explain it in the business plan itself. This information is provided on an as-needed basis. While you may not want all of this information available to everyone, having it available when creditors are looking to invest in your company can be beneficial, as it can help them make their final decision. If you are going to include an appendix in your business plan, you should include the following information:

- All credit history, both personal and business
- The resumes of all key managers
- Pictures of products
- Reference letters
- Marketing studies and research details
- All relevant book references or magazine articles
- Patents, permits or licenses
- Any legal documents you may have used

- Copies of relevant leases
- Any building permits you may have
- Preexisting contracts
- Business consultants, including your attorney and accountant

You should ensure that you keep a distribution record and control all copies of your business plan. Doing this makes it easier to update your business plan and maintain it on an as-needed basis. In addition to including all of these sections, you should also include a private placement disclaimer in your business plan if you intend to use it in order to raise capital.

Creating a well-structured business plan that covers all of the above sections in proper detail is imperative to helping you achieve your desired results. Whether you are looking to gain more employees, or are looking for creditors to invest in your company, you need to have a great business plan under your belt in order to make that happen. After carefully taking into consideration all of the above sections and filling them out properly, you should have an incredible business plan created for your company. This plan will be the foundation for everything your business does at this point, so it is really important that you make sure you are proud of your plan. Put in as much work as you need to in order to make sure that every section is filled out to the best of your ability and that the information is accurate and clear. The more professional and polished your business plan is, the easier it will be to acquire anything you need in order to start or grow your business.

Chapter 3: Tips and Tricks

Now you have an incredible business idea and a solid business plan. You have taken into account all of the sections that were discussed in the previous chapter, and everything is included. That is great! However, most people see business plans on a regular basis, and simply having a completed and thorough business plan is not enough to really impress them. This is especially the case if you are approaching creditors, who likely hear from businesses such as your own on a regular basis.

In order to really make your business plan pop in a way that is professional but still impressive and appealing, there are a few extra things you need to do and consider. By giving your business plan that extra one-over and making sure everything in it is absolutely outstanding, you give yourself the opportunity to stand out from the competition right from the get-go: the day you present your business plan. While many people will simply create a business plan and hope their idea is enough to impress the "judges", it can be a major benefit to have an incredible idea *and* plan to support you. In this section, we are going to explore all of the ways you can really make your business plan stand out, and help set you apart from the crowd.

While it is important to have all areas of your business plan filled out accordingly, it can be beneficial to emphasize on the key areas that investors and potential employees are most interested in. The more you are able to prove why your business will be a success and what sets it apart from the rest, the easier it will be for you to gain anything you wish to from your business plan. The following are specific areas that you should focus on emphasizing when you are creating your business plan:

1. Relevancy of your company: it is really important that you make it clear as to why your company is relevant and what need you are addressing. The clearer your creditors are on

your company's purpose and goal, the easier it will be for them to understand what you are asking for.
2. Market state and trends: if you are able to clearly and concisely convey the current state of the market, specifically in the targeted industry, as well as any relevant trends, it will be easier to back up any financial claims you make. This information is especially important for startup businesses to focus on, since they are relying on existing market information and not historical data derived from their own personal company experiences in the market.
3. Why customers will be interested: if customers aren't interested, no one will buy and your business will be a flop. Creditors and employees alike want to make sure they are signing with a company that is going to be reliable and stable. It is important that your products or services will attract ideal clients, and that those clients will actually like what you have to offer. The best way to fulfill this element is to look at the product or service from a customer perspective and address any issues or concerns that may arise from said viewpoint in advance, so you can perfect the idea *before* presenting it.
4. Detailed customer analysis: it is a good idea to be able to describe, in clear detail, who your targeted audience is. That is, what is their exact demographic? What is their psychographic? There are two questions that you will want to be able to answer specifically: who *exactly* is your customer? And, why are they buying your product or service?
5. Competitor analysis: you also need to be very clear on who your competitors are. Primary and secondary competitors alike need to be addressed and analyzed. The more you understand who your competitor is and *why* they are competitors (value, product, service, location, etc.) the easier it will be to set yourself apart from them and give great reasons as to why you will be successful in spite of their competition. In order to do this, you should be clear on

what these competitors advantages are and how you plan to offset their impact on your business.
6. Competitor displacement: knowing who your competitors are is going to help you when it comes to knowing how you will displace competitors, too. You should have a clear understanding as to who you are displacing, why, and most importantly: *how*.
7. Company offer: when you are describing your company's product or service, you need to be clear on what you are describing. Make sure that the person you are presenting to can clearly visualize what they are listening to. If possible, get a physical copy of the product into their hands and demo it for them. If it is a service, walk them through a scenario in which your service will be used and why it will be used. Give them a story from a customer's perspective and help them get in the mindset that really allows them to understand your product or service and its potential. If you are selling something that already exists, you also need to really highlight why yours is better than what is already out there. You should specifically list which brands you are up against, and clearly highlight why yours is better and how it will be more successful than what is already out there.
8. Resource overview: having a clear overview of the various resources needed to deliver the product or service is important. This includes anyone who is involved in the process of delivering the product or service, such as: sales force, marketing team, management, strategists, and more. It is important to outline everyone involved in making the entire process happen, and explain why they are important to the process itself.
9. Corporate priorities and achievement processes: in addition to describing your purpose and strategies, you need to clearly convey what your priorities are and how you intend to achieve them. Having a great idea and plan is effective, but you need to ensure that your creditors can understand your specific goals and where your priorities lie. This will

help them in making decisions regarding whether or not they will be offering you any funding. A creditor will want to agree with your intentions and ensure that your priorities are going to be activities that will assist you in making back their money, *not* potentially losing it.
10. Three financial plans: it can be a great benefit to include *three* financial plans instead of just one. These plans should include a conservative plan, a moderate plan, and an optimistic plan. Each should have realistic sales revenues, margins, expenses and profits that are achievable. You should convey them in monthly, quarterly and annual increments to help show people what your potentials are, and that you have considered all market conditions.

Chapter 4: SMART Business Planning

Now that you have all of this phenomenal information regarding how to plan your business, and what you need to involve in your planning, you may still be wondering how exactly you can set those goals. You've read words such as: *projected, conservative, moderate, optimistic,* and *historic data.* All of these words have revolved around your business goals and where you intend to take your business to in the next several months, and years. If you are a veteran in the business world, this may be easy for you: you already have witnessed business growth so you are very clear on how you can expect your own to go. However, if you're new to the business world, you may be having a hard time figuring out how to make *realistic* projections that creditors will actually believe.

A lot of your ability to create these goals are going to be based on market research and consumerism research that you will complete when you are creating your business plan. In addition to this research, it is important that you use SMART goal setting skills in order to create projections that will actually appeal to anyone you are presenting your plan to. This way, you are making others' clear on what *exactly* you expect to do, and when you expect to have it done by. When it comes to creditors and investors, they are going to want to ensure that you have very clear and specific goals set for your company and that you have intentions of reaching these goals. In order to implement SMART goals on your business, you can follow these instructions:

The SMART acronym stands for:
S – Specific
M – Measurable
A – Achievable
R – Realistic
T – Time-Scaled

Here is how the acronym works to help you create goals that any creditor will be impressed to hear:

Specific
Having specific business goals is important on many levels. First, it gives you a clear and focused direction in business. It allows you to know exactly what you intend to produce, where you want to be in your business, and what you will qualify as "success". Being clear on this information is also beneficial when you are hiring employees, as you can ensure you are hiring employees who are going to help you achieve these goals. They will have a clear idea of where your company is going, and will also be able to steadily work with your company goals in mind. Finally, having clear and specific goals allows you to clearly present to potential creditors where you plan to be in the next one to five years. This gives them an idea as to what exactly they are investing in, and why you need them in the first place. It also gives them proof that you have a focused intention and that you are not wasting their time or money on a plan with no clear goals in mind. Whenever you are setting goals for your business, you need to be very specific. Outline exactly what you are going to qualify as success, and make sure you share your intentions with anyone who is relevant to this process in your business.

Measurable
Being specific on your goals will greatly help you when it comes to having a measurable aspect to your goal. By having a measurable goal (such as: "we will raise $10,000 in one month" or "our sales will grow 15% by next quarter") you will be able to measure your success against the goal. This gives you a clear opportunity to see where your strengths and weaknesses lie, and how you can implement strategies that will strengthen your processes to help you meet your goals easier in the future. In addition, it helps you know if you have successfully reached your goal in that set time period. Finally, if you reach it and surpass it by a significant amount, then you know that you have set the bar too low and that in the future you should set your projections higher.

Achievable
Ensuring your goals are achievable are important. If you are setting goals that are too high, several issues are going to arise that will affect your business. Your employees will become discouraged, your creditors will likely realize you are being too optimistic in your goals and won't believe you are realistic in what you can achieve, and you yourself will feel as though you have failed. In addition, you don't want to have goals that are set too low, because once you achieve them you may not be as motivated to carry on higher. The best way to make sure your goals are measurable is to measure them against what you have already accomplished. If you cannot do that because you are a new startup, then you can measure yourself against the competition. Take into account the fact that they are already existing and have an established reputation, and that you will need to establish your place in the market still. This way, you can create achievable goals.

Realistic
As aforementioned, you need to have goals that are realistic. Before setting your goal in stone, you need to make sure it is realistic. If you can affirm that it is realistic, and that you are capable of doing it (either based on existing proof, or based on realistic projections) then you are ready to set your goal. In order to assess whether or not your goal is realistic, you should consider how large your goal is, and the amount of time you are giving your company to achieve it. For example, a brand new company with zero reputation and a fair amount of competition is not likely to make $100,000 on the opening day of their new store. However, if you have an existing major reputation, don't have a lot of competition in the area, and have already generated a large buzz, it may be realistic to state that in your first month you will achieve $100,000 in sales. How realistic your goal is will largely depend on what you have accomplished

already, or what the paralleled market has already accomplished in similar conditions.

Time-Scaled
It is imperative that all of the goals you set with your company are on a time scale. Having a time scale gives you a deadline to work towards, and allows you to make decisions that will move you towards this goal effectively. The time-scale on your goal should work in two ways. First, you should have a clear deadline as to when you intend to have achieved said goal. The achievement will be based on the success (or not) of your entire goal. So, if you intend to have 15% increase in sales in one quarter, then at the end of your quarter is your deadline. At that time, you can evaluate and reassess your goal and adjust it as needed. In addition to a deadline you should have set times at which you will evaluate your achievements. In a goal that spans over a quarter, you might consider having these reviews every week, or every month. This allows you the opportunity to assess where your strengths and weaknesses have been in achieving your goal, and strengthen them *before* the deadline comes along so that you have greater chances of success in your company.

Ensuring all of your goals follow the SMART goal planning strategy will allow you to ensure that all of your goals are successful. While you may not reach your desired success every single time, you *will* be able to easier address where the weaknesses in your strategies were. When you are able to establish where your weaknesses were, you can then implement new strategies to ensure you succeed in those areas next time. Then, you can reset your goal and work towards it! Ideally, your company should always be working towards a set goal. This way, you are consistently moving forward and up with your company, and you will be much more likely to continually achieve success. Companies who do not set goals, to not achieve greatness because they are not clear on what it is they have set out to achieve.

When you are creating your business plan, make sure that all of the goals you have made operate with the SMART strategy in mind. If you haven't already, review your goals and ensure all of the steps in SMART have been implemented. This will help you in many ways going forward.

SMART goals will:
- Help Your Company: having a clear vision of your goals and where you are going will help you make decisions that will lead your company towards your predetermined idea of success. If you are able to have a clear understanding of what it is you want to achieve, then you will know exactly what you need to do in order to achieve it.
- Help Your Employees: if you have a clear vision of what you are working towards, then so will your employees. Employees who are clear on what the company's goals are will be much more likely to work with these goals in mind and help your company reach these targets. Make sure that you always educate your employees on what your current goals are and how they can help your company achieve those goals.
- Help Your Creditors: when you are seeking funding, it is important to have clear, outlined goals. Creditors will want to see that you have specific goals in mind. They will also want to understand how those goals will benefit their repayment, and why they are relevant to the growth of your business. Ideally, your goals should be set with the intention of growing your business and earning greater profits each quarter, and year.

Chapter 5: The Purpose of Niches

You want to appeal to your market, but you have plans on how to appeal to them *all*. So, why not? If you can, why not appeal to every aspect of your market? You keep hearing that you should pick a niche, but why? Your service is so great, and *everyone* in that market can benefit. It really doesn't make sense to narrow your target and eliminate hundreds if not thousands, or even hundreds of thousands of potential clients! Why bother? You know best, right?

Wrong. Don't make that mistake. The reality is, people want to work with an expert. Let's focus on the medical industry: pretend you need a heart surgery. Are you more likely to go to a doctor who has done a little bit of everything, or are you going to go to a doctor who only performs heart surgeries? Likely, you will pick the doctor who focuses on heart surgeries. Why? Because they are an expert. They know what they are doing, and you can guarantee that if you invest your money, trust and time in them, that they are more capable of giving you your desired results versus the other doctor who may not know everything they need to know in order to successfully give you those same results.

The same is true when you are getting into business. If you have made your business plan with the intention of appealing to an entire industry market, it is time to evaluate your specific niche and then go back and reevaluate your business plan based on that niche.

Why You Need a Niche
There are many reasons why you need to focus on a single niche. Here are some of the most important ones:

Brand Yourself as The Expert
Just like with the heart surgeon example above, getting clear on your niche is important because it will help you become branded as

the expert. The more focused you get on the service you offer and the specific clientele you appeal to, the more you will be branded as the expert. For example, let's say you want to be a life coach. If you were branded as a life coach who deals with all of life, people would question your credibility. Who really knows enough about life to be a coach in *all* aspects? Probably no one. However, if you choose to be a life coach specifically for those who have recently emerged from a break up or a divorce, then you can become the expert in that field. People will come to you specifically for that need, and will trust that because that is the *only* criteria you focus on, that you will be amazing at helping them through that specific time. The more focused you get on who you want to serve and how you want to do it, the easier it will be for you to become an expert and provide the best service possible.

Increase Interest from Potentials
Again, referring back to the heart surgery example, if you brand yourself as the jack-of-all-trades style, less people are going to want to work with you. Instead, they are going to seek out the person who is an expert in what they are looking for. While picking a niche does eliminate the interest of those who do not fit your niche, it also attracts the interest of all of those who *do*. Instead of being disregarded by *everyone* because you are not credible and they are incapable of trusting that you will be able to offer the same quality of help as an expert, you will be regarded by the people you want to help most. Then, you will have access to your target audience and they will actually be interested in your services and will be much more likely to hire you, or purchase your products.

Reduce Number of Competitors
If you are working in an industry with a high number of competitors, having a niche can help eliminate that number. Realistically, every industry has a high number of competitors. Narrowing down can eliminate the need to compete with the entire

industry worth of competitors, and instead reduces your competition to only those who offer similar or same services or products as you do. At this point, your primary competitors will be those who offer almost exactly what you do, and your secondary competitors will be others in your industry. Having a niche really helps eliminate the number of people you have to compete against and increases your chances of being seen by potential clients. This is incredibly important, especially as a startup business, because people who are already established in the industry have a great advantage over you. Having a lesser number of competitors can actually be viewed as one of your company's strengths, depending on how few the number of competitors actually is.

Increase Growth Potential
The more you focus on a single niche, the more customers are going to come to you. This is because you will be able to market specifically to those unique customers, and therefore will have a much easier ability to attract them to your company. Additionally, your products and services will perfectly fulfill their needs, and so they will be more inclined to purchase from you. When this happens, you increase your growth potential exponentially. Rapidly, you will create loyal customers and attract new ones. The more focused you are on who you want to serve, the more you will be able to speak directly to that audience and form a relationship with them that will draw them in and help grow your business.

Reduce Major Business Expenses
For the same reason that it will enhance business growth, having a niche will also reduce business expenses. When you are speaking to a large audience with a variety of demographics and psychographics, you will need to invest a significant amount of money into marketing materials, as well as into valuable products and/or services that will fulfill all of their needs in a way that will actually encourage them to buy from you. If you are going to appeal

to an entire market, you will need to have set aside millions of dollars to market your company, and establish the services and/or products that they are seeking and will be willing to spend their money on. Unless you are a major company, it is likely that you do not have access to millions of dollars for marketing, product or service development, and employee growth and development. For that reason, having a niche will help eliminate the number of campaigns, products and services, and employees you will need in order to fulfill your purpose. If you have one specific target audience, you can establish marketing strategies that will speak directly to them, have products and services that focus specifically on their needs, and only hire the number of employees required to satisfy that amount of business. Then, if you desire, you can further expand into the rest of the market over time.

Eliminate Confusion
If you are not already clearly established or don't already have a reputation in the market, then not having a niche will increase confusion. Fellow businesses will not know what you are or who you are, creditors will have no idea what your intention is and will be less likely to invest in you, and customers will be less likely to visit you because they won't know what your purpose is. Having a niche allows you to have a clear, specified focus that is easy for everyone to understand. Creditors will be more likely to invest in you because they will clearly understand what it is you are achieving with your business, products and services. They will know that they do not have to invest hundreds of thousands of dollars into making your strategies effective because you are trying to appeal to too many people at once. As well, customers will know exactly who you are looking to appeal to, and the ones who fit your target audience description will be much more likely to visit your store and invest in your product or services. They will know that they are the ones who your products or services are tailored to, and then they will come to you to have those needs fulfilled. If your customers do not know that you are there to fulfill their needs, and

are unaware as to how you might even be able to do it – if you can even do it – then they are probably not going to take the time to come in to your store. Some may out of curiosity, but your overall impact will be diminished by the lack of clarity.

Establishing Your Niche
Now that you understand why you need to have a niche, it is time to figure out your niche if you haven't already. At this point, you may already be considering your niche. If you have already chosen one, that's great! If not, there are ways you can narrow it down to decide exactly who you want to serve. The following is a short list of things to consider when establishing your niche:

Consider Your Service
If you have made it this far in your business planning, you have likely already created an entire product or service for the market. At this point, you are very clear on what you have to offer and what need it will fulfill. An easy way to quickly establish your niche is to look at the market and get specific on *whose* needs your product or service fulfills. Is it targeted for people who just graduated? Brand new moms? Single dads? Young females from a specific geographical place? The more you understand exactly who your product or service is intended to serve, the easier it will be to decide your niche. Essentially, your exact ideal customer is your niche.

Be Distinctive and Specific
Once you figure out who your target audience is, it is time to get incredibly precise in your description. The following are some questions you can consider when you are figuring out who your dream client is:
- What age are they?
- What nationality are they?

- Where do they live?
- Why do they need your product?
- How will it benefit their lives?
- What are their buying habits?
- How can you appeal to them?

While there are many more questions you can consider, the aforementioned ones will help you start to get clear on who you want to serve. The clearer you are, the easier it will be to market to this specific audience and achieve great results in return.

Market Testing

Lastly, once you have picked a niche, you need to conduct some testing on the market to see if they actually need your product or service. Of course, in a dream world, every idea would be well accepted by the targeted audience and we would all succeed. Unfortunately, that is not reality and we must conduct market testing and market research in order to make sure that our ideas will actually be successful on the real market. Once you have gotten specific on your niche, you will need to conduct some market testing which can be done in several forms (soft launches, beta testing, surveys, etc.) and some market research. You can then go back to your business plan and implement this new and niche-specific information in order to make your business plan even more effective.

Having a clearly defined niche is going to give your business an incredible advantage. It will give you a stronger edge in the market, reduce your competition, increase your appeal, and ultimately assist you in having a successful business. The clearer you are on who you are talking to, the easier it will be to talk specifically to that audience. Having a niche will also help you when hiring employees because you can hire those who have skills and personalities that will appeal directly to your target audience and who will match your company "profile". Additionally, it will help you in getting creditors to invest in your company because they will not have to invest hundreds of thousands of dollars into helping you hire enough staff to sell an enormous number of products or services set to appeal to a high variety of people in the market. You reduce their risk by reducing your need for funding and make it easier for you to market your specialized products and services and find success in the market.

Conclusion

Thank you for reading "*Business Plans Template:* Learn the Simple Truth of How to Create an Effective Business Plan". This book was specifically designed with the intention of assisting any and all businesses with creating or updating their business plans to help establish a solid foundation for business growth. Whether you are looking to have a clearer action plan, hire new employees, or request funding, the information you have learned here will assist you in making a polished business plan that will get you the results you desire. A professional and well-researched business plan is important in any business, as it creates a sturdy foundation for all business operations to run from. The clearer you are with your action plan, the easier it will be to take action and achieve your desired results.

I hope that this book has made it easier for you to create your business plan. The information inside should be able to help you in creating a plan that will help you achieve any result you desire. Having a business plan that clearly takes into account all of your business ideas, history (if applicable), projections and goals is a great opportunity to establish your current position in the market and either enter or excel in a strategic way that will optimize your success. The more effort you put in to developing a strong business plan, the easier it will be for your business to establish itself or grow from where it already exists in the market place.

The next step is to brainstorm your exact business idea and put it on paper. Then, you can develop a clear idea on how you want to structure your business in order to create an action plan that will guarantee your success. From there, you can start developing your business plan with SMART goals. Finally, you can implement your business plan with whatever method needed in order to reach your desired outcome.

Lastly, if you enjoyed reading this book, please take the time to review it on Amazon. Your honest feedback would be greatly appreciated.

Thank you, and best of luck in creating your business plan!

www.ingramcontent.com/pod-product-compliance
Lightning Source LLC
Chambersburg PA
CBHW020713180526
45163CB00008B/3070